Exam FA1

Recording Financial Transac

Pocket Notes

AF891530

KAPLAN

PUBLISHING

British library cataloguing-in-publication data

A catalogue record for this book is available from the British Library.

Published by:
Kaplan Publishing UK
179 - 191 Borough High Street
London
SE1 1HR

ISBN 978-1-83735-287-6

Printed and bound in Great Britain.

Contents

Preface

These Pocket Notes contain everything you need to know for the exam, presented in a unique visual way that makes revision easy and effective.

Written by experienced lecturers and authors, these Pocket Notes break down content into manageable chunks to maximise your concentration.

Quality and accuracy are of the utmost importance to us so if you spot an error in any of our products, please send an email to mykaplanreporting@kaplan.com with full details, or follow the link to the feedback form in MyKaplan.

Our Quality Co-ordinator will work with our technical team to verify the error and take action to ensure it is corrected in future editions.

Introduction

In this chapter

- Overview of the examination.
- Keys syllabus areas.

Overview of the examination

The examination is a two-hour computer-based examination. It will comprise 50 two-mark compulsory multiple-choice questions.

As the examination is multiple choice only, you do need to consider the following:

- Multiple choice questions allow the examiner to cover a significant amount of the syllabus within each examination. This means you cannot simply learn only part of the syllabus and hope to achieve a pass standard – you will need to learn the entire syllabus to maximise your chances of success in the examination.
- Your question practice must be focused on multiple choice questions. As part of your revision, work through the questions in the study text and any question banks you may have to ensure you understand the style of question asked.
- Remember in the examination, you can answer questions in any order. It is therefore worth completing the easier questions first and then re-visiting the more difficult questions at the end of the examination. This approach will (hopefully) ensure you have obtained the easy marks first and avoid missing this should you run out of time.
- The multiple-choice questions will include both computational and non-computational elements.

Finally, when all else fails guess – there is no negative marking.

Key syllabus areas

- Business transactions and documents
- Double-entry bookkeeping
- The banking system and transactions
- Payroll transactions
- General ledger accounts
- Cash and bank transactions
- Sales and credit transactions
- Purchases and credit transactions
- Reconciliations
- Prepare the trial balance

chapter

1

Business transactions and documents

In this chapter

- Types of business.
- Accounting systems.
- Cash transactions.
- Key documents in credit sales / purchases systems.
- Other business documents.

Types of business

Types of business

Sole trader

- One person owns/runs business
- Entitled to all profit
- Suffers all loss
- Owners liable for business debts
- May have employees

Partnership

- Two or more people own/run business
- Profit split between partners according to their agreement
- Partners liable for business debts
- May have employees

Limited company

- Owners = shareholders
- Managers run the business
- Owners have limited liability – not liable for business debts
- In small company, shareholders may = managers

Accounting systems

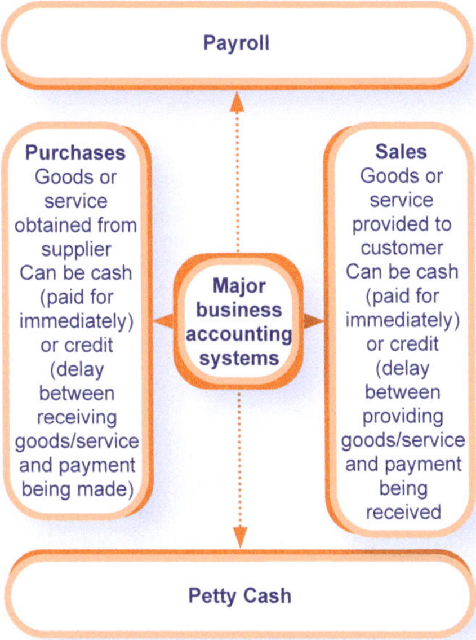

Key Point

- Accounting system used to record transactions.
- Many employees using accounting systems / ledger accounts.
- Control system therefore in place to ensure complete and accurate recording of transactions.

Reasons for producing business documents

- Evidence of the transaction and its details.
- Evidence of the stage that a transaction has reached (e.g. delivery note shows goods received).
- Check and confirm transactions made.
- Recording transaction details.

Cash transactions

Types of business

1. Over the counter sale

Cash or credit sale in shop. Customer given receipt to confirm transaction

2. Verbal order

Goods not yet available – order details written down on sales form for delivery when goods in stock

3. Telephone order

Order recorded on sales order form by company /goods dispatched to customer

4. Written order

Order form completed by customer – sent to company. Goods dispatched to customer

5. Internet order

Customer completes electronic order form on web site. May make payment on secure site. Goods sent to customer

Payment requisition

Situations

For abnormal expenses or payment requests not supported by invoice, e.g.

- deposit for catering services
- servicing of company car
- settlement of company credit card.

Process

1 Payment requisition form completed by manager and any supporting documentation attached.

2 Authorised by head of department.

3 Sent to cashier.

4 Payment prepared and made e.g. automated payment or cheque.

Key Point

Credit transactions

- Sales/purchases made with payment made later.
- Credit terms agreed – amount of time before payment is required and maximum amount of credit.
- Terms set by credit controller.
- Individual large orders may have own credit terms.

Key documents in credit sales/purchases systems

Sales system

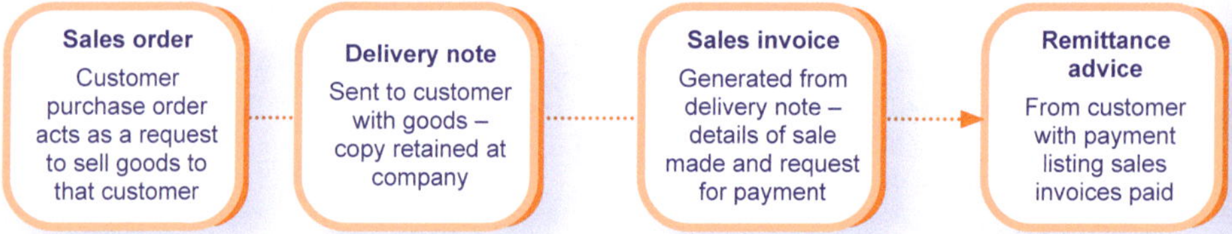

Purchase system

Documents – essential contents

Sales invoices/Purchase invoices

- Customer name and address
- Name of business, business address and telephone number
- Invoice number
- Invoice date
- Customer account reference
- Order number
- Goods: quantity, description, price
- Total invoice value
- Settlement terms

Purchase orders

- Business name of buyer
- Registered office and company registration number
- Supplier name and address
- Purchase order number
- Business contact
- Delivery date

Key Point

- Sales invoice sent from company to customer for goods supplied.
- Purchase invoice received from a company for goods purchased.

Other business documents

Statement of account
Sent monthly to customer showing invoices not yet paid

Credit note
Sent from supplier to customer, cancels part or whole of invoice for goods returned

Debit note
A document raised by a customer and issued to a supplier to request a credit note.

Petty cash voucher
Shows authorised expenditure from petty cash supported by documentation showing expense is genuine

Employee payslip
Notification to employee of wages earned less statutory and other authorised deductions

Contents of the payslip:

- employee's / employer's name
- date
- total gross pay split into elements e.g overtime, etc
- any employee pension contribution
- deductions from, or adjustments to, pay
- total gross pay to date
- total tax paid to date in tax year and tax due this pay day
- National Insurance/social security contributions due this pay day
- net pay.

Exam focus

Remember many of the multiple-choice questions on this section are factual so ensure you remember the names of the different types of business documents and what each is used for.

chapter

2

Principles and process of bookkeeping

In this chapter

- The process to record transactions in the accounting system.
- Accounting systems.
- Computerised accounting.
- Coding and processing of transactions.

The process to record transactions in the accounting system

Computerised bookkeeping uses same principles as manual bookkeeping. Double entry still performed – although printouts unlikely to be in 'T' account format.

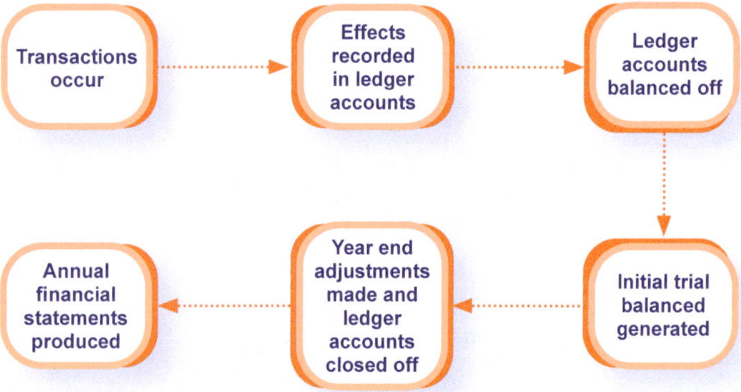

Accounting systems

Computerised bookkeeping uses same principles as manual bookkeeping. Double entry still performed – although printouts unlikely to be in 'T' account format.

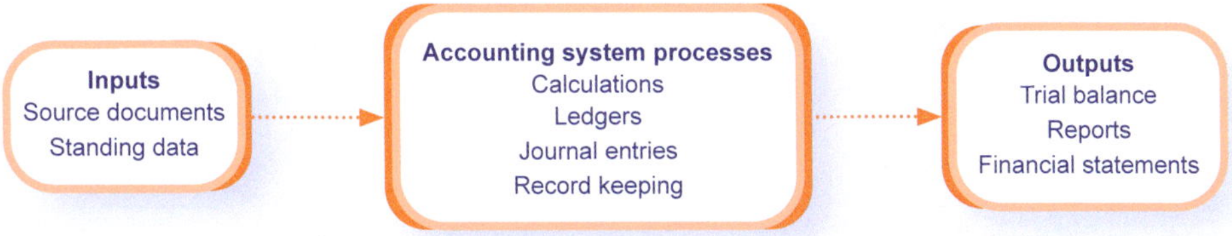

Computerised accounting

Computerised bookkeeping uses same principles as manual bookkeeping. Double entry still performed – although printouts unlikely to be in 'T' account format.

Advantages of computers	Disadvantages of computers
• Speed • Work from stored programs – needs fewer staff • Reliable – fewer mistakes than manual systems • Can be programmed to undertake complex decision making • Large amounts of data can be stored in very little space and retrieved quickly	• Lack of intelligence – cannot recognise errors or incomplete data • Relatively high initial costs • More difficult to amend computer programs than manual system • Makes organisation dependent on computer – more vulnerable to loss of resource • Can only make quantifiable not judgemental decisions

Cloud computing is access to software and data storage that is hosted on remote servers and is accessed via the internet. Cloud computing enables data and information stored to be accessed from any location at any time by multiple users if the user has an internet connection and can log in.

Cloud accounting is the application of cloud computing to accounting systems and processes.

Advantages of cloud accounting	Disadvantages of cloud accounting
• Ability to share and share data on demand • No maintenance or damage of physical server • Improved disaster recovery and data security	• Reliance upon the financial stability of cloud service provider • Risk of unauthorised access by service provider staff • Responsibility of service provider to comply with relevant law e.g. data protection

Cloud accounting applications

- A payroll bureau – to enable production of the payroll.
- An external accountant – to produce sales tax returns and the annual financial statements.
- Customers – to place orders and pay for goods ordered.

Coding and processing of transactions

Coding systems

All accounts should be given a code.

Sequential codes	Codes allocated in numerical order	0001 property 0002 motor vehicles
Faceted codes	Each digit signifies unit of information	3401: 3 = canned food 4 = soup 01 = Heinz
Mnemonic / significant digit codes	Codes include descriptive element off account in question	502828 – Jeans – 28" waist, 28" leg 503028 – Jeans – 30" waist, 28" leg
Block /hierarchical codes	Numerical blocks of codes allocated to certain types of accounts	0000 – 0999 non-current assets 1000 – 1999 current assets

Features of a good coding system:

- each item has unique code
- codes of uniform length/make up
- codes are significant
- index of codes exists
- scope for additional codes
- characters (commas, colons, etc) not used
- new codes authorised.

Exam focus

This section introduced the concept of double-entry bookkeeping. If you need to practise setting up 'T' accounts, please refer to the examples in the study text.

Batch processing

Batch processing of transactions takes place either at predetermined intervals such as daily or weekly or when a predetermined number of transactions is ready to be processed, for example 30 invoices.

Batch processing of transactions is primarily associated with manual accounting systems and processes.

Real-time processing

Real-time processing of transactions relates to computerised systems whereby processing of transactions is immediate. As soon as a transaction has occurred, the accounting system is updated.

Integrated computerised accounting systems will update all aspects of the accounting records and broader management information system as a transaction is processed. For example, as a sale to a a credit customer has occurred, the accounting system is updated, and there will be simultaneous update of the individual customer account records.

Exam focus

Note that the ACCA FA1 syllabus and exam assumes that businesses will be using an integrated computerised accounting system where the bank account is NOT part of the integrated accounting system. No knowledge of any particular computerised accounting systems or packages is assumed or required. The focus of the syllabus and exam is upon the processing of accounting transactions.

chapter

3

Double-entry bookkeeping

In this chapter

- The elements of the financial statements.
- The accounting equation.
- Income, expenses and profit.
- The financial statements.
- Accounts and ledgers.
- Double-entry bookkeeping.
- Balancing accounts.
- The journal.
- Trade and settlement discounts.
- Sales tax.

The elements of the financial statements

Key Point

An **asset** is a present economic resource which the business controls as a result of a past event. Examples of an asset used to generate future economic benefits are plant and equipment used by a business to produce goods to sell to customers, or inventory held for sale to customers.

A **liability** is a present obligation to transfer an economic resource as a result of a past event. This could be a bank loan or overdraft outstanding, or amounts owed to suppliers for goods and services received but not yet paid for.

Equity or capital is the amount due to the owner of a business after all liabilities have been paid. The owner has the residual interest in the assets of the business after all liabilities have been settled.

Income arises through increases in assets or decreases in liabilities that result in an increase in equity or capital. Examples include revenue from sales, bank interest received and fees or commission earned.

Expenses consists of decreases in assets or increases in liabilities that result in a reduction of capital due to the owner. Examples of expenses include repairs and maintenance, insurance and charges for heat, light and power.

Definition

- **Asset expenditure** refers to the purchase of assets for long-term use in the business (>1 year).
- **Revenue expenditure** is expenditure on expense items / goods for resale.

Asset expenditure may also be referred to as capital expenditure. Revenue expenditure may also be referred to as an expense.

Definition

- Assets for long-term use in the business are **non-current assets**.
- Assets for short-term use in the business are **current assets**. They include inventory, cash and receivables.

The accounting equation

Key Point

The accounting equation shows relationship between assets and liabilities in accounting system.

Definition

Business entity concept: A business is separate from its owners.

Any business always has:

- Assets – resources controlled
- Liabilities – amounts owed to third parties
- Capital – money introduced by owners

Assets
- Land and buildings
- Plant and machinery
- Motor vehicles
- Inventory
- Money in bank
- Receivables

=

Liabilities
- Payables
- Bank loan
- Bank overdraft
- Other payables (e.g. tax due to tax authorities)

+

Capital
- Amounts introduced to business by owner

- Elements change over time (e.g. when a sale occurs stock will fall and money in bank-increase)

Assets
- $2,000 Land
- $3,000 Inventory
- $1,500 – Money in the bank
- Total $5,500

=

Liabilities
- $1,500 due to payables

+

Capital
- $4,000 capital from owner

Income, expenses and profit

- Businesses sell goods and services

Definition

- Income = amounts received for selling goods and services
- Expenses = amounts paid to provide those goods and services
- Profit = excess of income over expenditure. Added to owner's capital (or deducted if a loss)

Key Point

Every transaction has two effects (the dual aspect). This means that after each transaction the accounting equation will still balance.

Income
- Sales of goods/services

–

Expenses
- Cost of materials used
- Salaries
- Telephone charges
- Rent
- Light, heat and power
- Interest on bank loan

=

Profit
- Surplus of sales over expenses paid
- Can be negative – indicates loss

The financial statements

The financial statements are based upon the elements of the financial statements and are a development of the information expressed in the accounting equation.

Statement of profit or loss – a summary of the income and expenses of a business for a period of time (e.g. a year) to determine the profit or loss made for the year. The profit or loss made for the period is transferred to the capital account of the owner in the statement of financial position

Statement of financial position – a statement of assets, liabilities and capital as at a specific date or point in time.

Accounts and ledgers

- An account is kept for each asset, liability income and expense item.
- Each account is given a code number.
- Accounts are kept together in the general ledger.
- General ledger also known as main ledge
- Each transaction is recorded once as a Debit and once as a Credit in two separat accounts in general ledger.

Account name and code

Date and reference	$	Date and reference	$
Debits		**Credits**	

Definition

Ledger = set of related accounts

Double-entry bookkeeping

A decrease in any balance is shown on the opposite side of account e.g. decrease in asset will be a credit entry.

Example

Purchase of motor vehicle:

- Debit motor vehicles account (increasing asset).
- Credit bank (decreasing the asset bank with the payment made).

Exam focus

Ensure that you are confident with which balances are debits and which are credits.

Questions focus on this.

General ledger – recording of assets and liabilities

Increase in debits	Increase in credits
Assets	Liabilities
Expenses	Income
	Owner's capital

Bank

		Motor vehicle	10,000

Motor vehicles

Bank account	10,000		

Balancing accounts

- Accounts closed ('ruled off') occasionally – each month or year.
- 'Balance' on account is carried forward to the next accounting period.
- Where debits > credits, account has a debit balance.
- Where credits > debits, account has a credit balance.

e.g

Example

Bank

Capital	5,000	Motor vehicle	10,000
Sales	10,000	Purchases	1,500
		Rent	2,500
		Balance c/f 31 Dec	**1,000**
	15,000		15,000
Bal b/f 1 Jan	**1,000**		

- Debit entries total $15,000; credit entries total $14,000
- Subtotals are made equal at higher amount of $15,000
- Balancing figure of $1,000 is inserted on credit side of account
- This is carried forward to become a debit balance at the start of the next accounting period

The journal

The journal – a record of accounting entries made to record non-routine transactions and to correct errors. Many journal entries relate to the correction of errors and accounting for issues relevant to preparation of the annual financial statements, such as writing off irrecoverable debts and updating the allowance for receivables. The journal may also be used to clear a temporary suspense account to complete the recording of a transaction.

Trade and settlement discounts

Trade discounts	Settlement discounts
Given to: • Regular customers • Customers buying in bulk ↓ • Given at point of sale • Calculated on price net of sales tax • Sales tax then calculated on price after discount given	Given to: • Credit customers ↓ • Given if payment received within stated time

Variable consideration

When goods are sold on credit, the seller must estimate the amount of revenue that will be receivable. Trade discount is always deducted in arriving at the price to be invoiced. If early settlement terms are offered to the customer, the seller must estimate whether or not it is probable that the early settlement terms offered will be taken by the customer.

If it is probable that early settlement will be made by the customer, then early settlement discount should be deducted in arriving at the invoice price.

If it is probable that early settlement will not be made by the customer, early settlement discount is not deducted in arriving at the invoice price.

When cash is subsequently received from the customer, any under- or over-receipt of cash (in comparison with the receivable recorded) is adjusted against revenue.

e.g

Example

A business sold goods to a customer on credit at a list price of $240. Early settlement discount of 4% was offered to the customer for payment within 7 days of invoice date.

If the customer is expected to take advantage of the settlement discount offered, the revenue and receivable will be recorded as: $240 × 96% = $230.40.

If the customer is not expected to take advantage of the settlement discount offered, the revenue and receivable will be recorded as $240.

Example

A business sold goods with a list price of $120 and offered a 5% trade discount to the customer. Sales tax is charged at 20%.

Net value of sales invoice $120 × 95% = $114

Sales tax: 20% × $114 = $22.80

Gross value of sales invoice:

$114 + $22.80 = $136.80

Exam focus

Exam questions often give you tax inclusive and exclusive amounts and require you to calculate the tax amount. Make sure that you are comfortable with calculations based on net and gross amounts.

Sales tax

Overview	VAT (sales tax) invoice
• Sales tax is a tax on the ultimate consumer • Collected by businesses on behalf of government • Charge sales tax on sales price • Pays sales tax on purchases • Sales tax charged at 20% (UK)	• Sales tax registration number • Tax point – date of transaction for sales tax purposes • Rate of sales tax • Amount of sales tax charged

Exam focus

This section introduced the concept of double-entry bookkeeping. If you need to practise setting up 'T' accounts, please refer to the examples in the study text.

chapter

4

Sales and sales records

In this chapter

- Sales invoices and credit notes.
- Stages in preparing a sales invoice.
- Recording a sales invoice.
- Recording sales returns.
- Statements of account.
- Aged receivables analysis.
- Communications with customers.
- Irrecoverable debts.

Sales invoices and credit notes

- For credit notes – obtain reason for credit and ensure goods returned prior to issuing credit.
- Credit note will also decrease amount of sales tax payable.

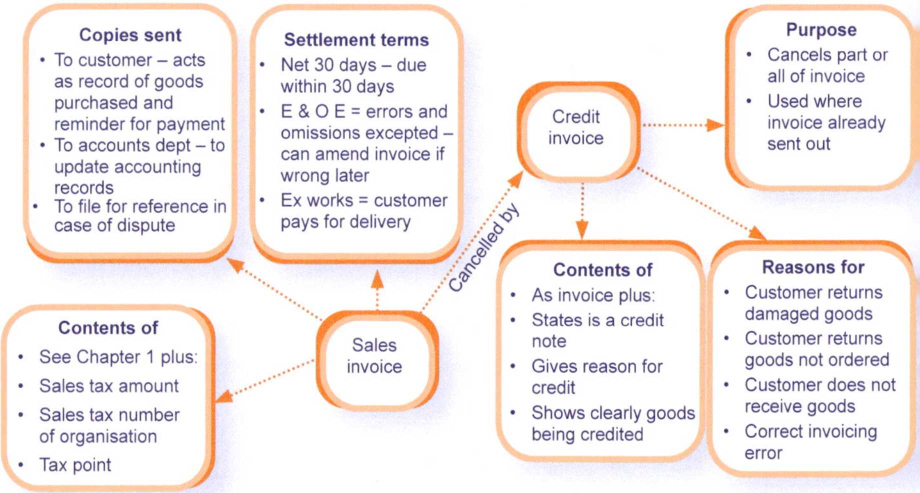

Stages in preparing a sales invoice

Authorisation
Relevant manager authorises preparation of invoice after goods/services provided

Preparation: Customer details
E.g. name, address and discount terms

Preparation: Goods details
Full description of goods sold including price

Checking
Checked against original documents (order etc) for accuracy

Sales invoices also coded with additional data, often a grid box stamp.

Code	Example	Reason
General ledger accounts	5003 / 4002	Show which ledger accounts sale posted to
Additions and calculations checked	✓	Confirm accuracy of invoice
Receivables ledger account number	J8762	Ensure invoice posted to correct customer account
Initial when posted	RGG	Confirm invoice posted to general and sales ledger

Recording a sales invoice

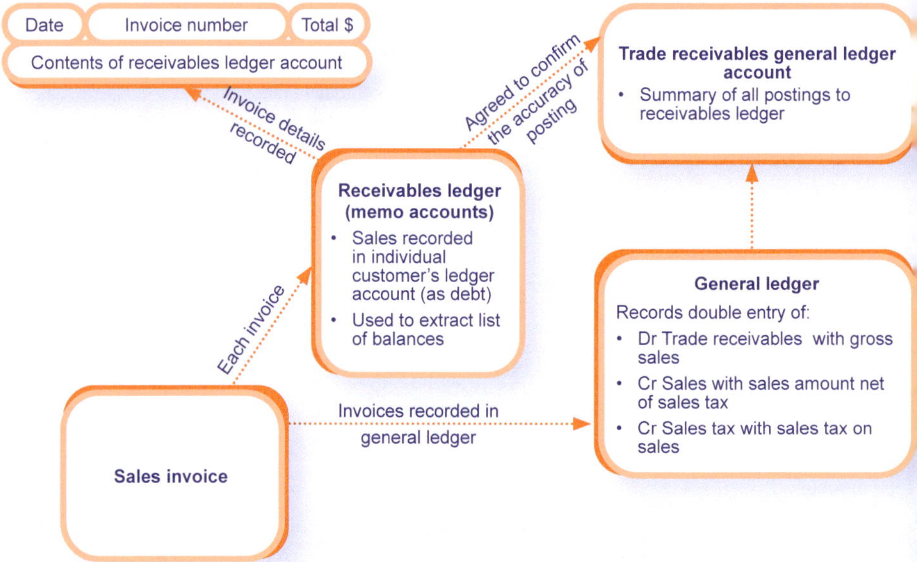

Recording sales returns

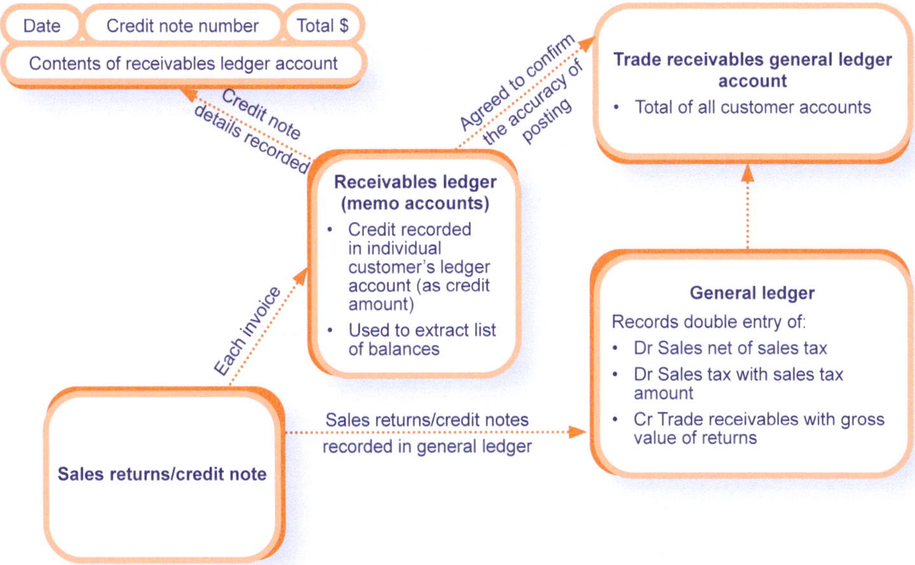

Statements of account

Explanation	Reason for producing
• Statement of transactions with one customer since last statement date • Shows balance b/f, all transactions (sales, returns, cash payments, etc.) and balance c/f • Extracted from individual sales ledger accounts	• Remind customers of state of their account (and request payment) • Record for customers of items purchased to check against their own records

Aged receivables analysis

Explanation	Reason for producing
• Shows analysis of amounts due from each individual receivable • Amount split by age of invoice (e.g. 0 to 30 days, 31 to 60 days…)	• Identifies customers with old outstanding balances for additional credit control procedures • Shows total aged receivable by month for management reporting. This identifies to management how efficient credit control procedures are

Communications with customers

Provision of credit	Setting credit limits	Chasing overdue debts
• Encourages sales • Ensures business remains competitive **Costs include:** • Funding working capital • Extra accounting system / staff • Performing credit checks • Operating a credit control function • Cost of customer defaulting • Legal costs of chasing debt	Limits based on: • Bank references • Supplier references • Creditworthiness computer programs • Interview with customer	Procedures include: • Send reminder letter • Speak to customer on telephone • Send final reminder letter • Refer to debt collection agency or solicitor

Irrecoverable debts

Irrecoverable debts are sometimes called bad debts. However, this is now old terminology.

- Amount due from customers unlikely to be paid.
- Main reason for – customer bankrupt.
- Recognise in accounts by removing the receivable balance and increase the irrecoverable debt expense account.
- Requires correct authorisation as debt removed from company's books.
- Relief for any unpaid sales tax may also be available.

Key Point

Remember that the individual customer accounts in the receivables' ledger are updated automatically at the same time as the general ledger accounts.

Irrecoverable debts expense account

Trade receivables	2,500		

Trade receivables

		Irrecoverable debt	2,500

chapter

5

Purchases and purchase records

In this chapter

- Ordering system.
- Checking purchase invoices and credit notes.
- Authorising and coding of purchase invoices.
- Recording purchases.
- Recording purchase returns.
- Aged payables analysis.
- Communications with suppliers.

Ordering system

Stages in ordering goods to obtaining purchase invoice.

Sales tax on purchase invoice

Check correct sales tax rate used and supplier's sales tax registration number on invoice.
Settlement discount offered – ensure sales tax calculated on goods value net of discount.

Checking purchase invoices and credit notes

Purchase invoice

Checks carried out – supply of goods

- Invoice agrees to purchase order
- Invoice agrees to goods received
- Correct prices charged 0n invoice

Treatment in accounts department

- Invoice, purchase order and delivery note matched and filed together
- Unmatched invoices, purchase orders etc filed separately awaiting other matching documents

Checks carried out – supply of services

- Invoice agrees to purchase order
- Invoice agrees to supporting documentation e.g. timesheet
- Correct prices charged and invoice casts correctly
- Lack of documentation – check invoice is 'reasonable' e.g. utility bill

Contents of

- See Chapter 1 plus:
- sales tax amount
- sales tax number of supplying organisation

Amended by

Credit note (from supplier)

Checks carried out

- Arithmetical accuracy
- Ensure for correct amount by comparison with original invoice

Purpose

- Cancels part or all of invoice
- Easier than amending invoice (already recorded in general ledger of supplying company)

Contents of

As invoice plus:

- States is a credit note
- Gives reason for credit
- Shows clearly goods being credited

Reasons for

- Return damaged goods
- Returns goods not ordered
- Invoice received but not goods
- Purchase invoice errors

Authorising and coding of purchase invoices

Methods of authorisation	Coding
1 Purchase invoice agreed to supporting documentation (e.g. GRN and Purchase Order) 2 Purchase invoice sent to official authorising expenditure, then signed by that person confirming invoice correct	All invoices coded with: • General ledger codes – ensure asset and expense differentiated • Supplier code for posting to payables ledger account

Purchase invoices also:

- Given sequential number to assist completeness of recording.
- Should have checklist attached to confirm all checks (e.g. agreed to purchase order) have been performed.
- Checklist may take the form of a grid box stamp.

Recording purchases

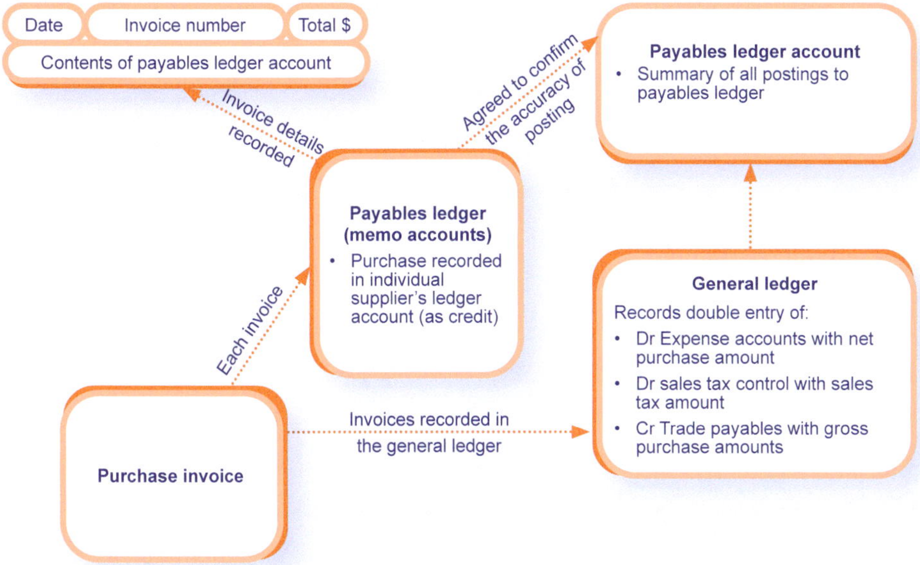

Recording purchase returns

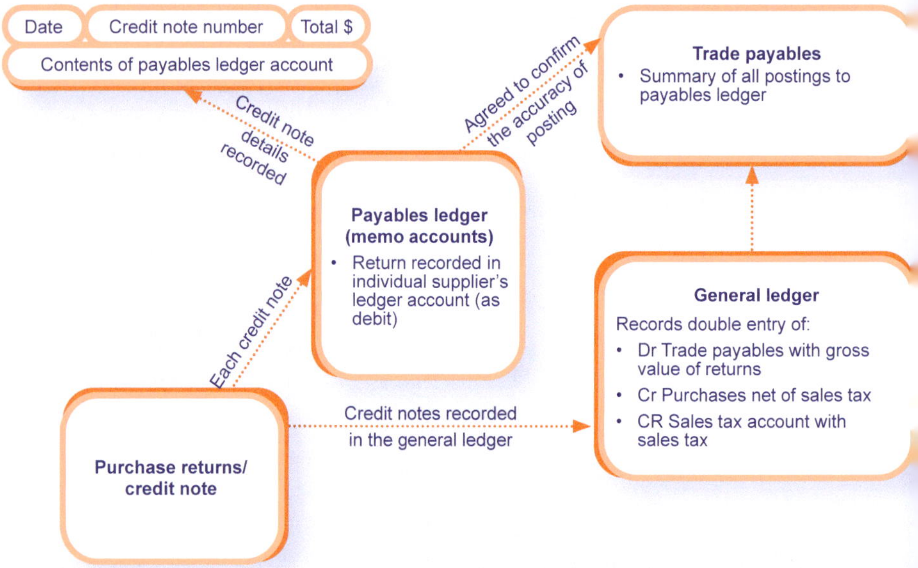

Aged payables analysis

Explanation	Reason for producing
• Shows analysis of amounts payable to suppliers • Analysis split by number of days each amount is outstanding	• Identify suppliers not paid – ensure paid promptly to maintain good supplier relations • Ensure settlement discounts are being claimed and not missed.

Communications with suppliers

- Communication focused on maintaining good supplier relationships and therefore continued supply of goods.
- Most communications relate to standard of goods received or reconciling supplier statements.

Exam focus

As with sales, you need to ensure you understand the double entry systems for purchases and returns. Refer to the activities in the study text if you need practice on these areas.

chapter

6

Recording receipts and payments

In this chapter

- Recording receipts.
- Recording receipts from credit customers.
- Cash payments.
- Bank-customer relationship.
- Clearing of cheques.
- Cheques.
- Credit and debit cards.
- Contactless payments.
- Security of cash/cheques.
- Reimbursement of employee expenses.

Recording receipts

Main sources of receipts:

- Cash and cheques from receivables.
- Cash and cheques from cash sales.
- Automated bank receipts from receivables.
- Credit card receipts from card company.
- Receipts from Internet site.

All entered into bank ledger account as shown on right.

Money received

Check against supporting information

- Cheque to remittance advice
- Credit card to vouchers
- Internet sales to credit card vouchers
- Cash to till roll

Prepare remittance list

- For cheques/ cash identifying customer account for each receipt
- Alternatively note receipt as cash sale

Cash and cheques only

- Bank paying-in slip completed
- Cash and cheques taken to bank

BACS transfer

- Money paid direct to company's bank account from receivable
- Also from internet where debit card used

Procedure

- Review bank statement when received to identify automated bank receipts
- Identify customer and amounts paid

General ledger

Enter receipts into general ledger
Dr: bank ledger account

Cr: Sales

Cr: Sales tax

Cr: Receivables

Recording receipts from credit customers

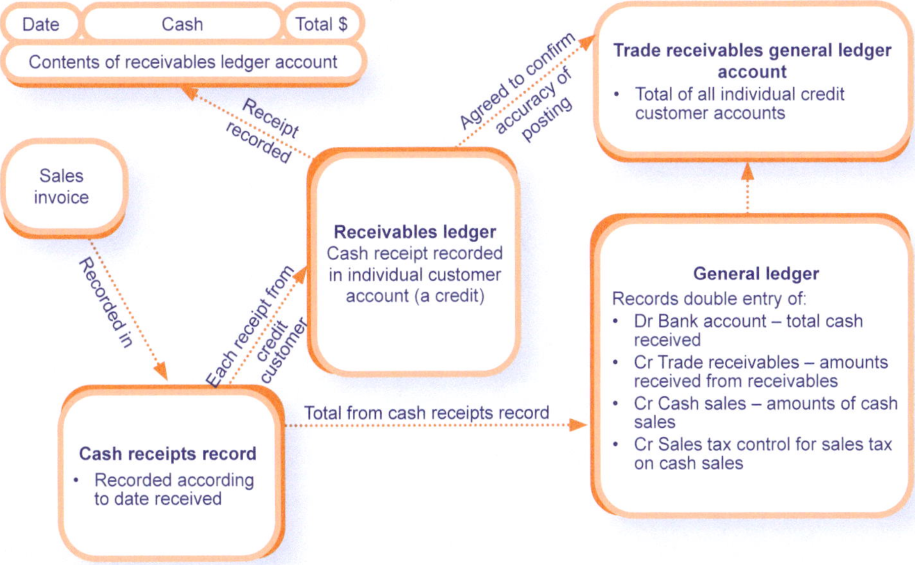

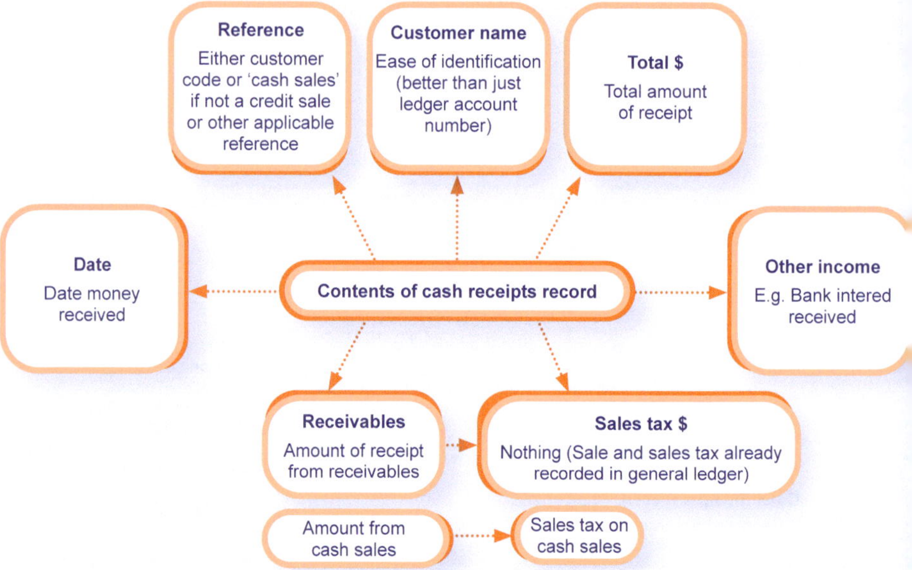

Note: Cash sales are assumed to be entered in the cash receipts record only, with the total split between the net sale value and sales tax amounts.

Cash payments

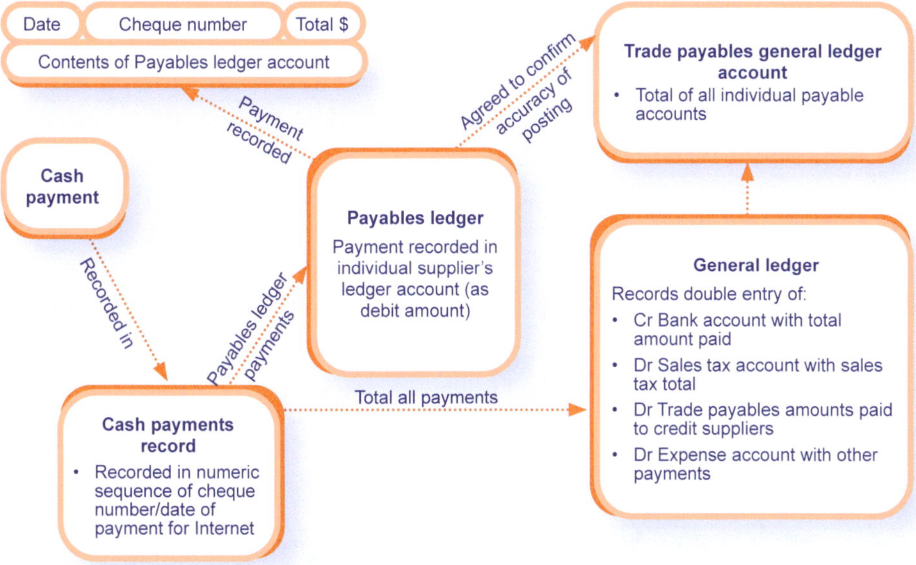

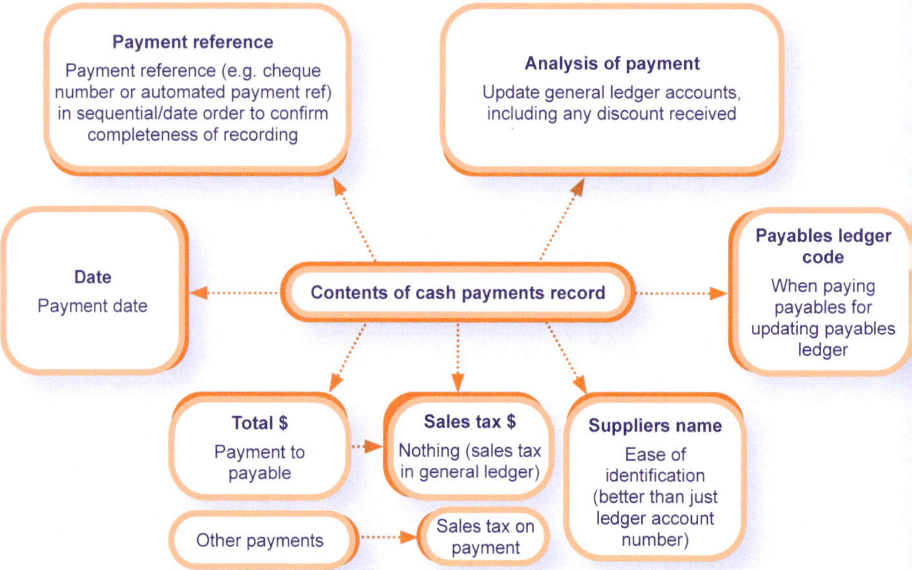

Note: Sales tax is only accounted for on payments not already in the general ledger. Invoices recorded in the general ledger will already have sales tax accounted for there.

Bank-customer relationship

Bank's obligations	Customer's obligations
• Pay cheques and other forms of payment on demand (up to balance in customer's bank account or overdraft limit) • Provide customer with balance on bank accounts • Provide statement showing transactions on bank account • Not to disclose customer information to unauthorised third parties • Use professional care in maintaining customer account	• Exercise reasonable care in drawing up cheques (e.g. not go overdrawn or forge cheques)

Clearing of cheques

Definition

Clearing of cheques is the process of paying in cheque and obtaining money due from that cheque.

1. Cheque paid into local branch of bank.
2. Cheques sent to Head Office.
3. Total amount of cheques due from other 'clearing banks' determined.
4. Net amount due paid to clearing bank's account at Bank of England.
5. Cheques sent to branch drawn on.
6. Drawer's account debited (assuming sufficient funds).
7. Dishonoured cheques returned to drawer.
8. Payee's account credited (following delay for clearing).

This clearing process can take up to three working days. More modern methods of automated payment have become more common.

Exam focus

Ensure that you know banking terminology.

Exam questions may ask what different methods of payment involve.

Cheques

(a) Bank name and branch
(b) Payee – person cheque payable to
(c) & (d) Amount in words and figures
(e) Date cheque written – after six months, bank will treat as out-of-date
(f) Bank sort code – unique to branch
(g) Name of account holder
(h) Account number
(i) Unique cheque number

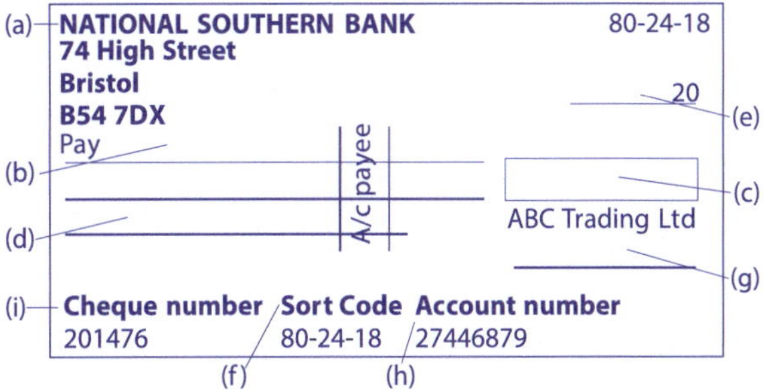

Cheque terminology	Bank account terminology
'**Crossed**' – two parallel vertical lines on cheque – payment must be made through bank	**Standing order** – transfer of set amount each month to the same payee
Endorse – pay a third party rather than initial payee – not possible if cheque is crossed	**Direct debit** – third party allowed to take varying amounts from payee, normally monthly
Cheque guarantee cards – bank guarantees payment of cheque up to card limit (cheque must be signed in presence of payee)	**Credit transfer** – Transfer to third party – with amount 'clearing' payee's account at start of transfer
	BACS = Banks Automated Clearing System – system banks use for above payments

Credit and debit cards

Credit cards

- Customer purchases goods on credit.
- Uses plastic card with magnetic strip or computer chip embedded in card.
- Latter = Chip and pin technology.
- Note charge cards different – full payment must be made each month – no part payments allowed.

Credit card

- Customer pays retailer with card
- Card company sends customer monthly statement
- Customer pays all or part of balance
- Interest paid on outstanding balance
- Card company pays retailer (less commission)

TIME

Debit card

- Customer pays retailer with card

Amount transferred from customer's bank account to retailer

Problems with cheques/credit cards:

Problem	Solution
1. Cheque incorrectly completed by customer	1. Send back to customer for amendment
2. Out-of-date cheque (> six months old)	2. Return to customer for re-issue
3. Credit card limit exceeded	3. Ask customer to pay by different method
4. Payment does not agree with supporting documentation (e.g. underpayment)	4. Inform customer – bank any monies sent and discuss remedial action with customer

Contactless payments

Contactless payments improve the speed and efficiency of making transactions by eliminating the need to sign a receipt or use a PIN number. The retailer needs to have an appropriate point-of-sale terminal. The customer can request a receipt and can also query the validity of any contactless transaction that appears on their bank or credit card statement.

They tend to be used for low-value transactions to minimise the risk of losses that may be incurred by card issuers or retailers if cards have been inappropriately used.

Security of cash/cheques

- Pay money into bank as soon as possible – minimises risk of fraud and theft.
- Keep cash and cheques in safe when on company premises.
- For large amounts of cash, consider using security firm to bank money – removes risk of individual being robbed on way to bank.

Exam focus

Questions on this area can be factual, e.g. how the banking system works, or more practical requiring knowledge of double-entry bookkeeping. More comprehensive examples of bookkeeping can be found in the study text if you need to revise this further.

Reimbursement of employee expenses

Problems	Solutions
• Claim not authorised in advance • Insufficient supporting evidence, i.e. no receipt provided • Claim exceeds employee's authorised limits	→ Refer claim to a higher level signatory than is usually the case. They should treat each claim on a case by case basis.

chapter

7

Petty cash

In this chapter

- Making a petty cash claim.
- Recording of petty cash.
- Reimbursement of petty cash.
- Reconciling petty cash.

Making a petty cash claim

- Normal claim process shown on right.
- Advances can be made – voucher amended to actual amount when receipt obtained – excess money repaid.

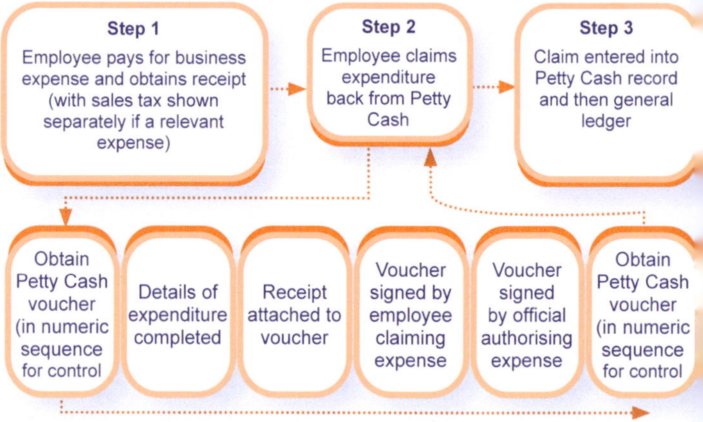

Authorisation

By

- Petty cashier, or
- Another responsible employee, or
- Petty cashier up to certain limit then another official

Procedure

1. Check amount does not exceed petty cash limits
2. Check claim supported by supporting documentation (sales tax receipt where relevant)

If no supporting documentation available, claim normally approved if 'reasonable'.

Security of petty cash	Problems with petty cash
• Kept in locked petty cash tin, preferably also in locked drawer or safe • Restrictions on number of people with key to tin	• Lack of supporting documentation – allow claim if senior person agrees • Claim exceeds petty cash balance – ask employee to complete standard expense claim

Recording of petty cash

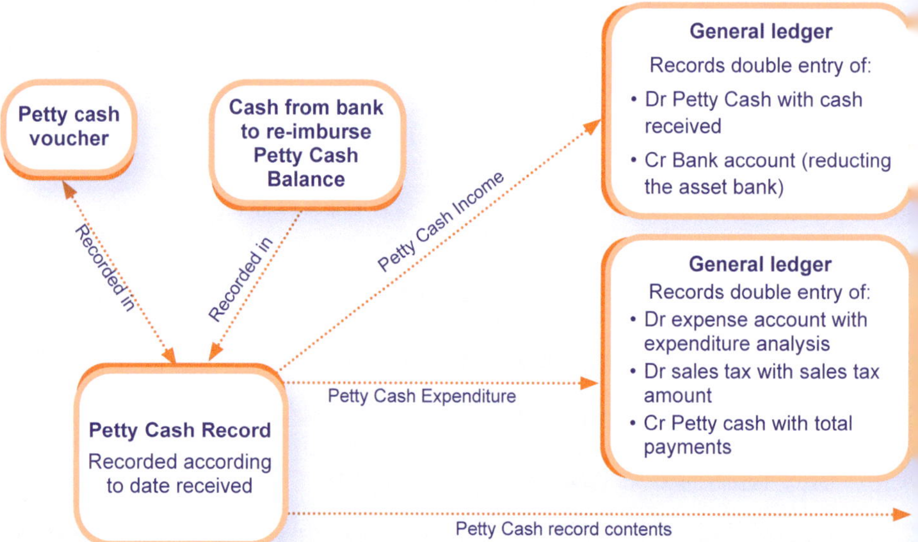

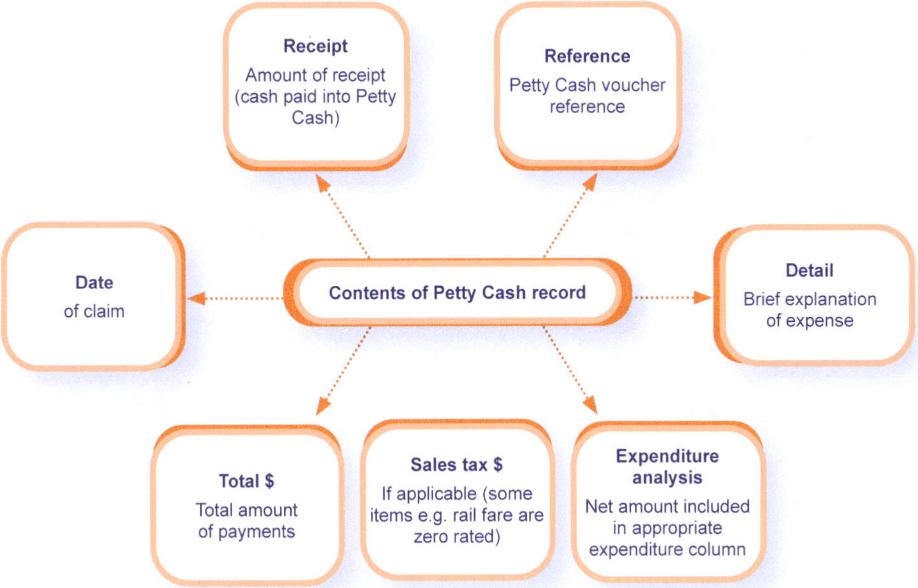
Receipt
Amount of receipt (cash paid into Petty Cash)
Reference
Petty Cash voucher reference
Date
of claim
Contents of Petty Cash record
Detail
Brief explanation of expense
Total $
Total amount of payments
Sales tax $
If applicable (some items e.g. rail fare are zero rated)
Expenditure analysis
Net amount included in appropriate expenditure column

Reimbursement of petty cash

Two methods of transferring money from bank account to petty cash account:

Imprest system	Non-imprest system
• Petty cash starts with given amount (e.g. $100) • Expenditure totalled over say two weeks • Exact amount of expenditure added back to petty cash; balance again $100	• Petty cash starts with given amount (e.g. $100) • Expenditure amount estimated as say $75 every two weeks • $75 added to petty cash every two weeks regardless of expenditure
Advantages • Petty cash always returned to same amount • Easy to monitor expenditure • Easy to check for fraud • Warns when petty cash reaching low level	Disadvantages • Large petty cash balance easily accumulates • Petty cash may run out if expenditure consistently underestimated

Reconciling petty cash

Reconcilation	Reason for petty cash not reconciling
• At any time amount of petty cash = imprest balance less total of vouchers / receipts in tin.	• Voucher not same as cash paid out • Incorrect amount of cash paid • Cash stolen

Exam focus

Ensure that you are familiar with the double entry of petty cash and how to calculate the imprest balance on a petty cash account.

chapter

8

Payroll

In this chapter

- Wages/salaries system.
- Basic pay calculations.
- Overtime, bonuses and commission.
- Authorisation and security.
- Accounting for payroll.

Wages/salaries system

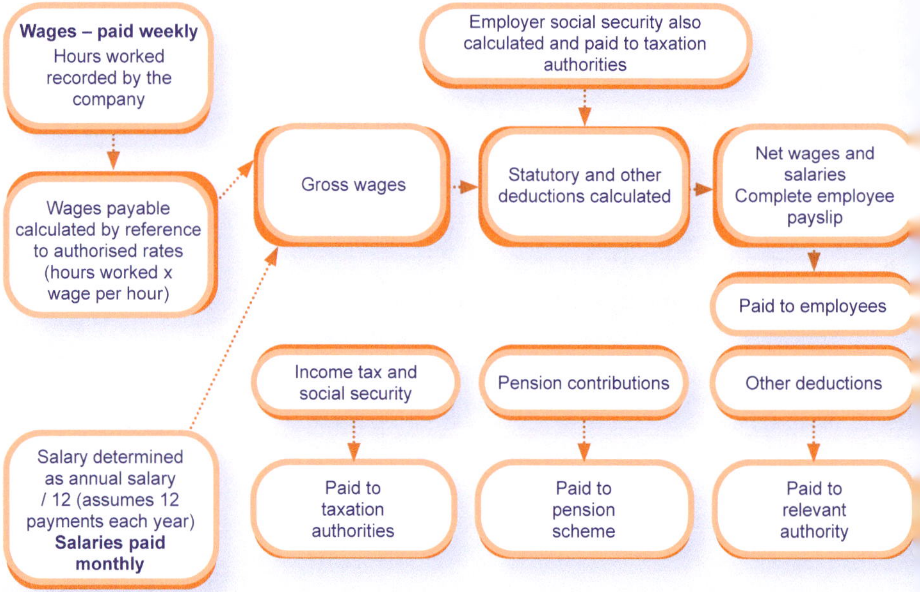

Key points with wages / salary system

- Cost of wages is gross salary + employer's social security (in UK) – other countries may have different regulations.
- Other non-statutory deductions made from gross pay can include:
  - Pension contributions
  - Payroll savings scheme
  - Trade union subscriptions
  - Voluntary deductions e.g. sports club membership.
- Wages / salaries paid by:
  - Cash
  - Cheque, or
  - BACS.
- Employee payslip must contain (by statute):
  - Employer's name
  - Employee's name
  - Date
  - Total gross pay and calculation
  - Employee's pension contributions (if any)
  - Other adjustments to pay
  - Total gross pay to date
  - Total tax paid to date and for this payslip
  - Net pay.

May also contain other information such as payroll number.

Basic pay calculations

Hourly paid employees	Piece rate employees	Salaried employees
Pay = Number of hours worked x hourly rate Hours worked recorded on: • Clock cards • 'Smart' cards • Time sheets	Pay = number of items made x rate per item • Can use differential rates (e.g. higher rate when produce above minimum number of items) • Guaranteed minimum wage – used if piecework wage is lower	Pay = annual salary divided by 12 (monthly pay) or 52 (weekly pay) • Normally paid monthly • Minimum number of hours to work each week, may be eligible for overtime

Overtime, bonuses and commission

Overtime – hourly paid employee	Overtime – salaried employee
• Amount worked over and above 'minimum' hours • Normally calculated at differential rate e.g. time and a half or 150% of the basic wage for overtime worked • Rate may vary depending on overtime hours e.g. 10 + overtime hours at double time	• Amount worked over and above 'minimum' hours • Not all salaried employees are paid overtime – check contract • Hourly rate calculated by dividing annual salary by 52 and then by the number of weekly contracted hours • The contract of employment may override this calculation

Definition

Bonus is additional amount earned if specific target met.

- For example, if output exceeds minimum amount or sales exceed minimum level.
- Paid according to bonus formula e.g. $10 for each unit made above minimum amount.

Definition

Commission amount paid to employee based on that employee's performance.

- Normally paid to sales staff as incentive to make sales.
- Often expressed as % of sales.
- Scheme may contain clause stating amount paid only when customer has paid (not just when sale made).

Authorisation and security

Authorisation	Security
• Authorisation needed for overtime to be worked and then to confirm has been worked • Authorisation of payroll needed to confirm accuracy of calculation and amounts to be paid • Authorisation normally: – Supervisor signs timesheet – Payroll 'signed' by senior accountant	• Payroll/salary information highly sensitive therefore must be kept secure • All information to be kept in locked filing cabinets or secure areas on computer systems • Uncollected cash wages to be kept in safe until claimed

- Split of personnel and payroll departments important.
- Compare personnel and payroll department records to identify 'dummy' employees and ensure employees who have left company are no longer paid.

Accounting for payroll

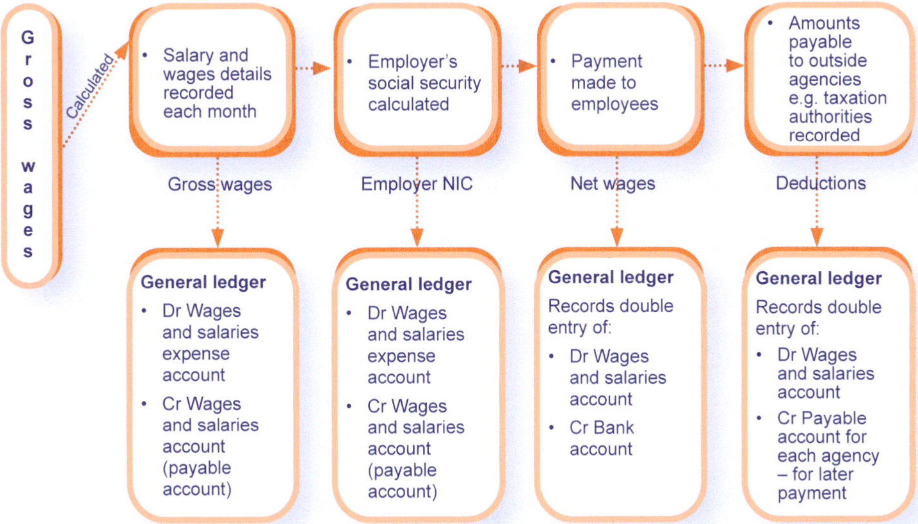

Overall effect:

- Wages and salaries account has zero balance.
- Wages and salaries expense account shows total wages/salary cost including employer's NIC.
- Bank account pays net salaries and all deductions to appropriate agencies.

Exam focus

Ensure you understand the different methods of calculating gross wages and salaries. Worked examples are included in the study text if you need them.

chapter

9

Reconciliations

In this chapter

- Need for bank reconciliation.
- Preparing a bank reconciliation.
- Example bank reconciliation.
- Supplier statements.
- Supplier statement reconciliations.
- Preparing a supplier statement reconciliation.
- Example supplier statement reconciliation.

Need for bank reconciliation

Bank reconciliation needed to:

- Check accuracy of the bank ledger account by agreeing balance to independent source.
- Identify bank ledger account error = Entering receipt or payment incorrect (wrong amount).
- Identify bank ledger account omissions = Items on bank statement not yet in bank ledger accoun

Reasons for bank ledger account omissions include:

Item	Explanation
Dishonoured cheques	Customer's bank does not honour cheque (normally due to insufficient funds in customer account)
Credit transfers	Customer paying direct to company's bank account
Direct debit	Actual amount of direct debit not known until after it has occurred
Bank charges	Notified by bank in arrears

- Bank reconciliation explains difference between balance shown in bank ledger account and balance shown on bank statement.
- Produced after most errors and omissions above have been rectified.

Main reconciling items are then:

Item	Explanation
Cheque payment	Delay between sending cheque to supplier and supplier banking cheque
Deposits	Delay between entering deposit in bank ledger account and deposit clearing the bank

Preparing a bank reconciliation

- Sequence of preparation shown on diagram.
- In step 2, matching items normally evidenced by ticking the bank ledger account and bank statement.
- In step 2, the previous bank reconciliation is needed to identify items entered in the bank ledger account in March that did not clear the bank until April (as shown on the next reconciliation).

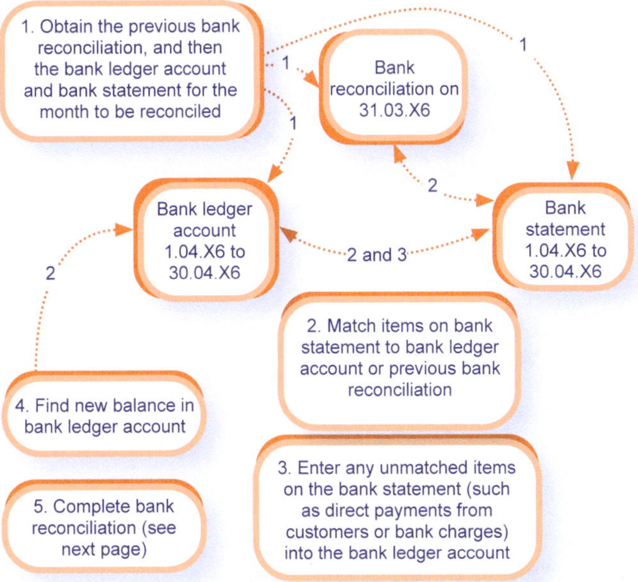

Example bank reconciliation

- Unpresented cheques are payments in bank ledger account but not yet at the bank. Deducted from bank balance.
- Outstanding lodgements are deposits in bank ledger account but again not yet at the bank. Added to bank balance.

"Unticked" items in bank ledger account

From bank statement

From bank ledger account

Bank reconciliation statement as at (date)		
	$	$
Closing balance in the bank statement		3,451.00
Unpresented cheques		
Cheque 13578	45.00	
Cheque 13580	291.00	
Cheque 13583	138.00	
		(474.00)
		2,977.00
Outstanding lodgements		
Receipt VBF Limited	200.00	
Receipt S Dowding	37.00	
		237.00
Closing balance in bank ledger account		3,214.00

Exam focus

Most examination questions in this area focus on explaining reconciling items on a reconciliation and finding new bank ledger account balances. Ensure you can identify reconciling items and calculate revised bank ledger account balances.

Supplier statements

Key Point

- Received each month from suppliers.
- Shows transactions with their customer (the purchasing company).
- Balance should agree to individual supplier account in payables ledger.
- Supplier statement and ledger balance may not agree due to items such as:

  1. Cash in transit (cheque issued but not yet received at supplier).
  2. Invoices not recorded (goods received but invoice not yet received by customer).
  3. Arithmetical errors.

- Therefore supplier statement reconciliation carried out to identify reconciling items and correct errors.

Supplier statement reconciliations

A monthly statement often sent by suppliers which lists movements on the account. A suppliers' statement reconciliation can then be performed as an additional check that all transactions have been recorded.

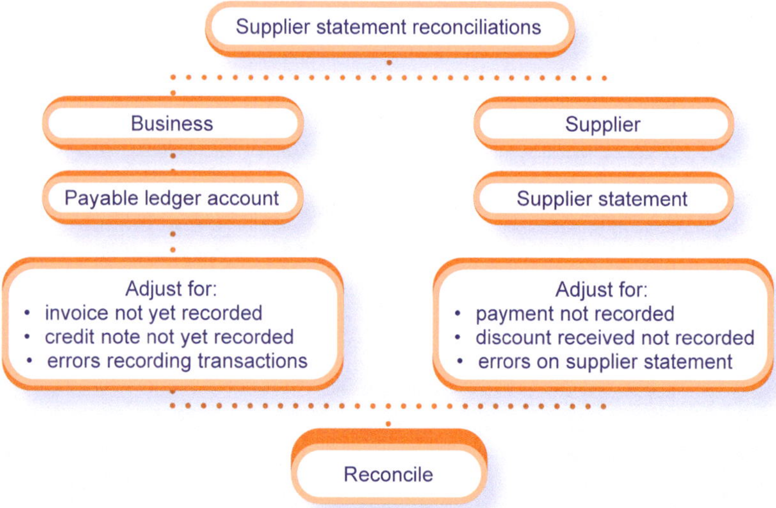

Exam focus

Questions dealing with reconciliations may require you to derive the relevant general ledger account balance, or to calculate the statement balance.

Preparing a supplier statement reconciliation

- Sequence of preparation shown on diagram.
- In step 2, matching items normally evidenced by ticking the bank ledger account and bank statement.
- In step 2, the previous supplier reconciliation is needed to identify items entered in the bank ledger account in March that did not clear the bank until April (as shown on the next reconciliation).

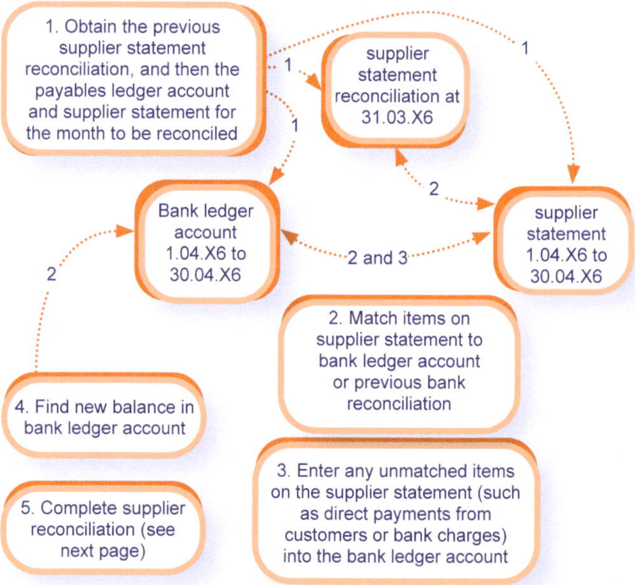

Example supplier statement reconciliation

- Unpresented cheques are payments in bank ledger account but not yet at the bank. Deducted from bank balance.
- Outstanding lodgements are deposits in bank ledger account but again not yet at the bank. Added to supplier balance.

"Unticked" items in bank ledger account

Supplier statement reconciliation as at (date)		
	$	$
Closing balance in the supplier statement		3,451.00
Unrecorded payments		
Cheque 13578	45.00	
Cheque 13580	291.00	
Cheque 13583	138.00	
		(474.00)
		2,977.00
Invoices not on payable ledger		
Invoice 2348	200.00	
Invoice 2593	37.00	
		237.00
Closing balance in bank ledger account		3,214.00

From supplier statement

From bank ledger account

Exam focus

Most examination questions in this area focus on explaining reconciling items on a reconciliation and finding new bank ledger account balances. Ensure you can identify reconciling items and calculate revised bank ledger account balances.

chapter

10

The trial balance

In this chapter

- Producing a trial balance.
- Errors in producing a trial balance.
- Errors identified by a trial balance in a manual accounting system.
- Errors not identified by a trial balance.
- The suspense account.
- Correcting errors – clearing suspense account.

Producing a trial balance

Key Point

- Starting point for the preparation of profit and loss account and statement of financial position.
- Shows current balances on all accounts – useful for management.
- Helps identify errors in accounting records.
- The process noted below explains the procedures to produce a trial balance. In a computerised accounting system, this would normally be produced automatically when required.

Producing a trial balance

1. Balance all accounts in general ledger.
2. List balances of all accounts separating debit and credit balances as shown on right (some headings e.g. assets will have more than one entry in a 'real' trial balance).
3. Total debits and credits – they should be the same.
4. Where debits do not equal credits, investigate and find reason(s) for discrepancy.

Balances on a trial balance

	Dr	Cr
Assets	$	
Liabilities		$
Capital		$
Drawings (from capital)	$	
Income (sales)		$
Discounts received		$
Purchase returns		$
Expenses	$	
Sales returns	$	
Irrecoverable debts	$	
Should be the same! ····►	**Total**	**Total**

Definition

Trial balance = list of balances extracted from the general ledger.

Errors in producing a trial balance

Key Point

- Mistake in finding balance on account in general ledger.
- Mistake in drafting trial balance (e.g. account omitted from list of balances, or debit balance placed in credit column).
- Note that the ACCA FA1 syllabus and exam presumes that computerised accounting systems are used to record transactions. Therefore, errors that would result in recording an unequal value of debits and credits in the general ledger are unlikely to occur.

Errors identified by a trial balance in a manual accounting system

Error	Example
Amounts for one transaction recorded differently in two ledger accounts.	Motor vehicle purchase recorded as $10,500 debit in the motor vehicle account and $10,050 in the bank account.
Transaction recorded as two debits or credits rather than one debit and one credit.	Motor vehicle purchase recorded as a debit in the motor vehicle account and also a debit in the bank account.
Error of single entry.	Motor vehicle purchase recorded as a debit in the motor vehicle account. No other entry is made.

Errors identified by trial balance debit and credit totals being different.

Errors not identified by a trial balance

Key Point

- The error examples below may occur in both computerised and manual accounting systems as there will be an equal value of debits and credits recorded in the general ledger.

Error	Example
Error of commission Correct amount entered into wrong account.	Sales invoice for D.Kay entered as debit in ledger account for K.Dee. Correct by credit to K.Dee's account and debit to D.Kay's account.
Error of principle Correct amount entered but in wrong 'class' of account.	Amount for a motor vehicle repair entered as a debit in motor vehicle account (treating the expense as an asset addition). Correct by credit to motor vehicle account and debit to motor vehicle repairs account.
Error of omission Transaction not recorded in the accounts at all.	Purchase invoice omitted from general ledger accounts. Correct by entering invoice into general ledger accounts.
Transposition error Debit and credit amounts for one transaction entered incorrectly.	Sales invoice for \$1,030 entered as \$1,003 in both trade receivables and sales accounts. Correct by debit of \$27 to trade receivables and credit of \$27 to sales account.

Error	Example
Compensating error One error cancelled by another of same amount.	Debit on rent account understated by $50, but debit on light and heat account overstated by $50. Correct by debit of $50 to rent account and credit of $50 to light and heat account.
Error of original entry Original transaction entered incorrectly in accounting records.	Purchase invoice for $560 entered as $580 in both the purchases account and the payables account in the general ledger. Correct this by debit of $20 to payables account and credit of $20 to purchases account.
Complete reversal of entries Debit entered as credit and visa versa.	Cash sale recorded as debit to sales account and credit to bank account. Correct by debit to bank and credit to sales account for double the amount of the sale.

Ensure that you know what types of error affect the trial balance, and what types do not. Exam questions may explicitly ask you to distinguish these, or you may need to know for the purpose of correcting a suspense account.

The suspense account

Key Point

- Used in a manual accounting system when debits and credits in the trial balance are not equal.
- Balance on suspense account = difference between debits and credits in trial balance.
- Trial balance therefore 'balances' by including the suspense account in list of balances.
- If have suspense account, next activity is to clear that account.
- In a computerised accounting system, the suspense account may be used as a temporary account to record one part of a transaction whilst seeking further information or clarification of that transaction. Upon receiving that information, the suspense account can be cleared with the the transaction fully and correctly recorded.

Correcting errors – clearing suspense account

Type of error	How to clear
Error causes an imbalance between debits and credits in accounts e.g. amount for one transaction recorded differently in two ledger accounts.	1. Identify ledger accounts affected. 2. Identify which ledger account(s) have incorrect balances. 3. Determine the amount of the error. 4. Determine whether a debit or credit is needed to clear the error. 5. Enter a corresponding debit or credit in the suspense account to complete the double entry correcting the initial error. 6. Ensure that the correcting entry is recorded in the Journal.
Error does not cause an imbalance between debits and credits in accounts e.g. it is an error of commission or omission.	1. Correct the error as outlined in the section on 'errors not identified by the trial balance' earlier in this section. 2. Remember that the suspense account will not be affected by this amendment. 3. Ensure that the double entry is recorded in the Journal.

Exam focus

Some of the more challenging examination questions involve the clearing of a suspense account balance. Try to follow the procedures outlined above for each error found, being very careful to get the debits and credits of the correcting entry right. There is a worked example in the study text if you need practise in this area.

Index

N

O

P

R

S

T

V

W